Just Enough to See

poems by

Betty Les

Finishing Line Press
Georgetown, Kentucky

Just Enough to See

Copyright © 2023 by Betty Les
ISBN 979-8-88838-146-5 First Edition
All rights reserved under International and Pan-American Copyright Conventions. No part of this book may be reproduced in any manner whatsoever without written permission from the publisher, except in the case of brief quotations embodied in critical articles and reviews.

ACKNOWLEDGMENTS

Grateful acknowledgment is made to the publications in which the following poems first appeared, sometimes in a slightly different form:

"State of Grace" in STOLEN LIGHT
"The Weekend News," "Just Enough to See," "The Invitation," "Pale Morning Dun," and "Safe" in AND YET
"Close" in *2014 Wisconsin Poets' Calendar*
"Old Friends" and "Salt" in PHOENIX: OUT OF SILENCE…AND THEN
"Little Miracles," "Fire Moon," "White-fronted Geese," and "Boulder Field" in BEYOND DISTANCE
"Falling Away" in CROW: IN THE LIGHT OF DAY IN THE DARK OF NIGHT
"A Single Leaf" in REVERBERATIONS: A VISUAL CONVERSATION

Thank you to Fran Claggett-Holland and Les Bernstein for their generous mentoring and support. This chapbook would not have happened without them. Critiquing by the Blue Moon Poetry Collective was invaluable. Special thanks to my husband, Anthony Les, for making sure I never got lost along the way.

Publisher: Leah Huete de Maines
Editor: Christen Kincaid
Cover Art: *Beech Forest*, Anthony J. Les
Author Photo: Jessica Les
Cover Design: Elizabeth Maines McCleavy

Order online: www.finishinglinepress.com
also available on amazon.com

Author inquiries and mail orders:
Finishing Line Press
PO Box 1626
Georgetown, Kentucky 40324
USA

Table of Contents

State of Grace 1
The Weekend News 2
Twilight 3
Elephants 4
Sphinx Moth 5
Close 6
Old Friends 7
Just Enough to See 8
The Invitation 9
Altered State 10
Moonlight Sonata 12
Shiny Little Rocks 13
Slippery 14
Pale Morning Dun 15
Black Earth Creek 16
Little Miracles 18
Fire Moon 19
Safe 20
When Trees Talked 22
White-fronted Geese 23
Salt 24
In and Out of Fog 25
The Properties of Water 26
Falling Away 27
And the Redbird Sings 28
This Kind of Extraordinary 29
A Single Leaf 30
Let the River Talk 31
Boulder Field 32
Eclipsed by Stones 33
When the Horses Came 34
Always the Birds 35

State of Grace

The big Douglas firs
show me the way
their lower limbs
bare and brittle
bleached white with age
arcing downward
toward the Earth
like birds
coming in
for a
landing

The Weekend News

The Arctic is burning
Sao Paulo dark with smoke
Icelanders mourn a beloved glacier
world leaders struggle with the
consequences of "unprecedented"

I try to shake off the ache of it
go outside to watch morning light
when a tiny pearl appears
at eye level beside me
suspended in mid air

I blink look closer
a spider comes into focus
dangling from a strand of silk
the sun catching it just so
turning its flesh-colored body
opalescent white

I stand watching
as the spider
so small in this big world
continues downward
headfirst
toward solid ground

Twilight

A feeling sweeps over me
so sweet
I can hardly bear it

everything seen differently
perfectly

I stumble outside to get a grip
listen to the crickets
rubbing their spiny wings together

their music pulses
through me
I hold onto a lawn chair

so I don't
fly away

Elephants

outer space must be
a very busy place
what with souls rising
right and left
day and night

imagine the traffic

if there is any negotiation
when my time comes
I'd like to travel in the
company of elephants

their big ears
flapping silently
their tiny eyes
catching starlight

Sphinx Moth

I knew everything would be okay
when I spotted a sphinx moth cocoon
wedged into a crack
where the stucco met the
wood frame of my front door

I talked to it relating
how sphinx moths
visited my garden back home
nectaring like hummingbirds
on bee balm at twilight

Towhees ambled into
my kitchen pecking
crumbs off the floor
hummingbirds
flew into the dining room
sending tiny bejeweled feathers
down onto my plate

A swarm of bees rested
outside the front windows
a great horned owl called
from the eaves of the roof

I knew everything would be okay
when I felt a tremendous urge
to shed my clothes
tugging at my shirt
an image of the moth
floating in front of me

I dashed to the front porch
looking for the cocoon
now broken open
empty
a beautiful sphinx moth
drying its wings
on the lip of the mailbox

Close

What's good about friends
is being out somewhere
maybe in the country
or anywhere really
and seeing something
that catches your eye

A lighted barn on a dark night
stained glass in a sagging eave
a low patch of irises
greener than grass

Whatever.
It's knowing the sight
is penetrating the other
at just the same angle
without saying a word
or even looking to see
the soft edges
of their smile

Old Friends

It's all in the noticing
what's there or not
what we perceive
what we are open to perceiving

The human eye is a tricky organ
so influenced by the brain
and then there is the heart
which swings open and shut

It took me five years
looking at the rock formation
five years of being drawn to it
touching it studying it

Before I saw the smooth gray
drape of skin
elephantine body and legs
the well placed eyes

Two old friends
one slightly turned toward the other
sharing a private thought

Just Enough to See

> *On Viewing "Monet, the Later Years"*
> *at the de Young Museum of Art, San Francisco*

It was his painting of the
bridge in bright reds
deep browns and greens
that did it
dabbed and slashed
across the canvas
like a storm

I confess I never liked
Monet's bridge
the Japanese tea bridge
he painted so often
arching like an interruption
over his exquisite water lilies

but it is always good
to see something anew
to be delightfully surprised
especially when you
think you know everything
about yourself

the bridge invisible
except for the mere
hint of an arch
just enough to imagine it
just enough to long for it

as Monet must have done
cataracts closing in
head still on fire
ushering in a new way
of seeing

The Invitation

Canyon de Chelly National Monument

I could have easily missed it
not wandered down to the far end
or turned my gaze away
at the crucial moment

Worse
I could have seen it
dismissed it
too unlikely
too otherworldly
but that's not what happened

It was early spring
we had the place to ourselves
Spider Rock jutting up
from the valley floor
brilliant red sandstone
against clear blue sky

I imagined Spider Woman
atop the rock weaving
her sacred web of connections
while streams cut the canyon
and the Dineh walked into the world

Deeper into the canyon
I noticed the ravens
two of them flying along the rim
tossing something between them
catching it in their beak
tossing it back to the other

I stood still mesmerized
as the ravens passed closer
closer to the canyon wall
closer to me

Then the juniper sprig
landed at my feet
raven catching my eye
as it made the toss

Altered State

Mt. Katahdin, Maine

In the predawn darkness
peering up at the park ranger
directing us to a different trail
the difficult trail
I offered "how bad could it be"
my husband looking at the map
turning the car around
withholding comment

He knew how bad it could be
I should have too, but
I was in an altered state
arriving to this spot
directly from my father's
funeral in Texas
still pondering eternity
still suspended in time

It was one of those situations
designed in heaven or hell
we couldn't put off the hike
my daughter was finishing
the Appalachian Trail
all 2, 200 miles of it
and it ended at the top
of the mountain

It was easy going at first
a moderate ascent
the sunrise energizing
the mountain solid

I did not worry
as the morning wore on
even when the trail steepened
even when the trail disappeared
into huge boulders with iron handholds
the drop-off dizzying
and me afraid of heights

I did not worry as we
slowed our pace
registering remotely somewhere
that I was tiring
that we were nowhere near the top
that I would have to hike
back down the mountain too

The "top" came into view over
and over, encouraging us
fooling us, until I woke up
to my situation and said
"This time it's got to be the top
I just can't go on"

And it was the top
there was my daughter
looking down at us
nothing between us except
mountain, air, and sky

I straightened myself
not knowing what reserves
to call upon when I felt
an invisible hand on my back
a gentle wind lifting me forward
the light turning a golden yellow

I've pondered that moment many times
was it my daughter's powers
pulling me to the top
my father
the mountain
the universe

and how
can I get back
to that
altered state

Moonlight Sonata

Waking to *Moonlight
Sonata* so soft
I couldn't be sure
if it was the radio
or a dream
the music seeming
to play inside me
through me

the joy I felt at twelve
playing it on the piano
how the music took me places
I couldn't yet comprehend
making me feel young and old
at the same time

I thought about other music
certain pieces
that seemed to be old friends
even at first hearing

Pachelbel's Canon
such joyful sorrow
Delibes' Flower Duet
sublime beauty
Beethoven's Ode to Joy

as I grew up
these stirrings
were just ripples
in a stream of observations
but now that I am grown old
I wonder

where do these feelings
come from
and what happens
to the music we love
when we die

does it die with us
or float on the night air
like a mockingbird's song

Shiny Little Rocks

It used to be physicists
were the only scientists
willing to think
outside the box
moving closer to God
in quantum leaps

now I'm happy to note
biologists are leaping too
or at least some are

venturing that humans
are not the only animals
who appreciate beauty
have particular ideas
about it
preferences

There's more.
They say this appreciation
is no small thing
has driven evolution
has shaped our world
shaped us

the extravagant splendor
of the natural world
the beauty we wake up to
cannot be explained
by usefulness alone

This is all encouraging
going in the right direction
but my god we've been
slow to catch on

the shiny little rocks
washed up on the beach
have been whispering
these truths and more
for eons

Slippery

Rounding a corner
in my neighborhood
I see my daughters
when they were seven and five
waiting for me at the bus stop
standing alongside their bikes
in the shade of street trees
their smiles reshaping my day

Waking to a Sunday morning
half asleep half awake
I tell myself
I think I'll call Mom and Dad
see how they're doing
sipping coffee in their den
in the coolness of morning
before the Texas sun overtakes
their day

Never mind my daughters
are grown
my parents dead twenty years
as is the way of time
in my world

Pale Morning Dun

Observe the mayfly
Ephemerella
pale morning dun
crawling out of her body
emerging from the water
to a beautiful spring day

she rests in alder shrubs
hardening her wings
producing her eggs
waiting
for the ancient call
to join the swarm
to mate

she flies low over the water
depositing an egg
here and there and there
until she is spent

is it sad
or profound
such beauty
so brief
a lifetime in three days

what is time but relative
human life a heartbeat
compared to a redwood
compared to a rock

Black Earth Creek

Near Madison, Wisconsin

Water
sheeting through
wet meadow
past Red-winged Blackbird
and Sora Rail
flowing almost imperceptibly
downward until it reaches the creek
my favorite creek
at the old railroad bridge

that night the moon was full
I crept to the creek
hoping to see *Hexagenia*
huge mayflies, so profuse
trout go crazy feeding on them
smacking the water as they rise
over and over

standing without flashlight
eyes adjusting to the dark
I looked by chance toward
the opposite bank
where the creek bends
leaving a deep hole
of slack water

just at that moment
a huge brown trout
poked its head
soundlessly out of the water
taking a long look around
its eye catching the moonlight
its snout a perfect arch

I held my breath
four heartbeats passed
then it was over
the moment

caught and sealed
the big brown
poking its head out
the creek flowing through us
in the dark

Little Miracles

When I look back at summer
the summer of sickness and doubt
shootings and rage
institutions crumbling
earth's systems buckling
fires beyond our worst imaginings

I want to remember the bluebirds
nesting in the hollow of
the old walnut tree at the end
of my block

I discovered their nest
when I walked by one day
and heard chirping
baby bird chirping
coming from inside the tree
then noticed the brilliant blue
and orange birds overhead
making shorter and shorter
circles toward the hole

I moved on just enough
to put them at ease
watching as plump caterpillars
and succulent berries were
delivered into the hole

how rich I felt
how much bigger my life seemed

I checked on the tree everyday
imagining the nest inside
a cup of finely woven grasses
perhaps feathers and bits of fur

I was there when the bluebirds fledged
just happened to be walking by
if such a thing can be happenstance
watched them perch on the lip
of the hollow one by one
and take the leap
of their lives

Fire Moon

Santa Rosa, California

It was beautiful
rising above the trees
full and round
just as I anticipated

except for the color
like a National Geographic
sunset in Tangiers
or the way molten steel
glows as it's poured
from a blast furnace

fires are burning at the
edge of my town
burning all over the state
turning the moon orange
filling the night with fear

yet here I am
standing in the middle
of the street
ashes collecting on
my face and shoulders
gazing at the moon
trying to hold on
to wonder

Safe

I wanted to write about Amal
the Yemeni girl dying of starvation
her portrait published in the Times
five days before she died

I wanted to write about how
she had no muscle no fat
just bone
skin draped over bone
over ribcage
protruding
like ripples in a pond

I wanted to write about
how her face
was serene
turned to the side
sparing me accusation

I wanted to write about how my
heart caved in on itself anyway
how my legs went weak
as I saw all of humanity
go over the cliff

I wanted desperately to capture all this
at the very least
bear witness to her suffering

But when I started to write
a different poem came out
a poem about the time
I was camping in Montana
how I was up before daybreak
wrapped in a blanket
waiting for the sun to come
over the mountains

How I saw a doe pass in front of me
stepping deliberately towards
the river bottoms

how she came back with her fawn
hidden all night in the willows
licked clean of scent

How they headed up the
hillside together
disappearing into the spruces
to forage

How that memory shelters me
the doe always coming
the fawn always safe

When Trees Talked

There was a time
when trees talked
humming *it's all right*
when we climbed down
from their branches
we'll always be here

and they were there for us
providing refuge
solace
wisdom
for thousands of years

that was when we were small
knew the sacredness of trees
knew we are part of
something much bigger

we are still small
but we don't know it
we look at the landscape
and see only ourselves
now we cut down the trees
shouting jobs
money

because there are so many
of us and we have forgotten
how to listen
or the trees no longer bother
with creatures so lost
so broken

White-fronted Geese

It wasn't the familiar
hronk honk of our local Canada
it was like the distant
sound of children laughing
boisterous and wild

high above me
receding to the north
geese lots of them
making their way
through the dark

I listened
awestruck and small
until the sky held only the
memory of their calling
their journey

piercing the night
wings pumping
eyes resolute
heading toward the right stars
a certain magnetic tug
born knowing
their true north

Salt

We are born
with the taste of it
on our lips

salt from that
inland sea

is it any wonder
we spend our lives
seeking the ocean
to feel again

the salt spray on our face
weightless
floating and rolling
the sense of belonging
imprinted
on our limbs

In and Out of Fog

North Bay, near San Francisco

I think about life
what humans strive
to understand
how to love
without conditions
how to fully forgive
the joyfulness of sorrow
the darkness of night

driving along Highway 37
skirting San Pablo Bay
so close to the water
I can smell the sediments
hear the *keek keek keek*
of the Black-necked Stilt

mudflats come into focus
then fade
the view across the bay
whole cities and ships
appear
disappear

how it seems I will
never get there
insights
appearing
disappearing
in and out
of fog

The Properties of Water

I take the small blue cup
from the bathroom shelf
run the faucet
until the water warms
shake in some salt
watch it swirl and dissolve

Water is the universal solvent
I hear Miss Smith say
blushing beet red
as she did every day
while we strapped on our goggles
lit up our Bunsen burners
setting off to explore
the properties of water

I take the warm water into my mouth
swirl it around, gargle, spit, repeat
I do this every morning
a repetitive unconscious act
yet today my yoga teacher's sutra
echoes in my ears
what do you want to let go of
what do you want to embrace

I think about what happened
in that small blue cup
the sodium splitting off
from the chloride
moving toward the water molecule
how this happens all around us
in our world
in our bodies
making life possible
seamless transformation

I finish the last swish of salt water
run my tongue over the warm
smooth interior of my mouth
ease into the question
what do I want to let go of
what do I want to embrace

Falling Away

what happens when
a species goes extinct
a polar bear
a seahorse
a bird

ecologists tell us
a thread comes loose
falls away
weakens the fabric
of our existence

but do we also know it
inside
feel it in our depths

the pieces of our soul
falling away

the pieces that knew
the dense wooly fur
of the undercoat
the tiny heart pulsing
through transparent body
the rush of warm air over
outspread wings

the pieces that were the bear
the seahorse
the bird

falling away

And the Redbird Sings

Ann Arbor, Michigan

I stick a hand out of
the covers
check the clock
five a.m.
right on time

Only the redbird knew
what to do
sheltering in the barberry
for the night
making his way up
to his perch on the sweet gum
before first light
grasping the ice-laden branch
belting out his spring song

The February ice storm
threw us into tumult
searching for flashlights
candles
pulling on coats
foraging a cold supper
from the darkened fridge
curling under comforters
uncertain
waiting for dawn

Outside
the wind rattles
darkness lingers
and the redbird sings

This Kind of Extraordinary

Madison River, Montana

I went for a walk after dinner. I wasn't expecting anything extraordinary, just taking in the evening air in the long light of summer, wandering down toward the river through sage brush. But you never know when extraordinary is going to happen. As I walked further into the meadow a White-crowned Sparrow flew toward me, landing just three feet away, its delicate pink feet straddling two twigs of sage. I thought surely he would fly, being in such an open, exposed position and given me, standing there, breathing the same air. But he didn't. Just looked at me and preened while I took in his magnificence. The snow whiteness of his crown stripes, the faint black tip of his beak, the delicate checkering on his wings, the tiny feathers encircling his eyes. I went back the next evening, scanning the meadow, wanting more. No luck, of course, not for this kind of extraordinary.

A Single Leaf

From the Exhibition "Reverberations"
Sebastopol Center for the Arts

In the end
if we are lucky
we come round to nature

Mapplethorpe did
and in his coming round
he gave us the leaf

inviting us to look
really look
as if it is the only thing
that matters in the world
the only thing that exists
in that moment

inviting us to see
perfection
in its sensuous curves
the delicate tips of
its upper margins
the intricate Vs
of its venation
pointing downward
a chain of hearts

connecting leaf to limb
limb to trunk
to sun and soil
to tree
gracing
a favored view

to Mapplethorpe
holding the leaf
against a window pane
catching the light
just so

Let the River Talk

North Umpqua River, Oregon

We sit among treetops
Douglas fir
big leaf maple
white alder
the river far below

not much is said
the trees or us
content with observing
the way the morning light

turns everything rose gold
the way the wind shifts
up canyon
in the afternoon

mostly we leave the talking
to the river
shooting aquamarine
out of the canyon

plunging over
rounded river rock
smashing
into ancient basalt
roaring its story
up to us

Boulder Field

Above Lake Abert, Eastern Oregon

It begins with water
collecting in cracks
freezing and thawing
freezing and thawing
like hammer and wedge
on hard basalt

until pieces cleave off
rumbling down the hillside
coming to rest
here and there
like swinging statues
holding a pose
for the next thousand years

while bright orange lichen
slowly encrust their surface

Eclipsed by Stones

it really does help
to get away
not just anywhere
though
there must be stones

look for mountains
high and rocky
sheltering a valley
with a little cabin
near a river
full of stones

go outside
sit among stones
carried by glaciers
think about how long
ago that was
and yet the stones
are still there

listen to the river
especially at night
tumbling over stones
rounded by time
it will tell you
all you need to know

don't worry about
Lake Mead going dry
leaving millions
without power
don't think about the heat
burning up the West
the floods imperiling the East
don't think about hunger
poverty and death

everything you dragged
with you
eclipsed by stones

When the Horses Came

Texas Hill Country, Near Leakey

The horses came in the night
ghostly under a pale moon
nuzzling my cheeks
sniffing my hair
nickering softly
as I reached up to
touch them
their breath sweet
and moist on my face

Always the Birds

In the Venn diagram
of my life
birds are in the middle

lifting me up during the thin
carrying me higher in the thick
the fine details of their beauty
their mystery
holding me together

water is there too
flowing through me
the deep consciousness
of water
the river beneath the river
the creek beneath the creek

the silence
it is there
when I am with the
birds and the water

my heart pulsing
to the same beat
the beat at the center
of the circles

the beat of the birds
always the birds

Betty Les was born in Texas and spent her first years in an old farmhouse under the canopy of a sprawling live oak tree. She felt a pull to nature early on, roaming the limestone hills, spring-fed creeks, and mesquite plains of her home landscape.

Betty graduated from the University of Texas with a Master's in Zoology, then joined the Peace Corps, carrying out studies on large river systems in Colombia and Ecuador. She went on to work as a zoologist in the Midwest helping to conserve species and ecosystems. These were eye- and heart-opening years as she learned just how connected everything is and how nature can be an opening to larger mysteries.

Betty turned to poetry to explore her experiences, at first scribbling thoughts that welled up onto scraps of paper and tossing them into a shoebox. Her writing accelerated when she moved to California and was invited into a critique group of active North Bay poets under the mentorship of poetry icons Fran Claggett-Holland and Les Bernstein and began a practice of daily writing.

Betty's poems have appeared in Redwood Writers Anthologies (*And the Beats Go On, Stolen Light, Phoenix, Crow, And Yet, Beyond Distance, and Crossroads*), in *Reverberations: A Visual Conversation* published by the Sebastopol Center for the Arts, in *The California Writer's Club Literary Review*, and in other works. Betty was selected as an Award of Merit Poet in 2018 and is a member of the Blue Moon Poetry Collective.

Through simple observations and a spare form, Betty's poems capture the profound that exists all around us. Among her work, you'll find poems on extinction, birds and insects, the deep presence of rivers and trees, and the consciousness of rocks. Her poems also explore the intersection of nature and the human condition, addressing themes of home, memory, beauty and loss.

Betty lives in Santa Rosa, California.

www.ingramcontent.com/pod-product-compliance
Lightning Source LLC
Chambersburg PA
CBHW022123090426
42743CB00008B/977